3 x 21 (2008)

...cbeth

...or Kids

by Lois Burdett

A FIREFLY BOOK

Published by Firefly Books Ltd.
Copyright © 1996 Lois Burdett

Seventh Printing, 2007

Library of Congress Cataloging in Publication Data available.

Canadian Cataloguing in Publication Data

Burdett, Lois
    Macbeth for kids

(Shakespeare can be fun)
ISBN-13: 978-0-88753-279-5 (pbk.)
ISBN-10: 0-88753-279-9 (pbk.)

1. Children's plays, Canadian (English).* 2. Children's poetry, Canadian (English).* 3. Readers' theatre.
I. Shakespeare, William, 1564–1616. Macbeth for kids. II. Title. III. Series.

PR2878.M3B87   1996   822.3:3   C96-900262-9

Published in Canada by
Firefly Books Ltd.
66 Leek Crescent
Richmond Hill, Ontario
L4B 1H1

Published in the United States by
Firefly Books (U.S.) Inc.
P.O. Box 1338, Ellicott Station
Buffalo, New York 14205

Printed and bound in Canada by
Friesens, Altona, Manitoba

OCT 1 6 2008

Canadä

The Publisher acknowledges the financial support of the Government of Canada through the Book Publishing Industry Development Program for our publishing activities.

Robert Wilson, © *Kitchener Waterloo Record*

Back row (left to right): Eric Schiek, Julian Hacquebard, David Marklevitz, Alex Fitzpatrick, Lois Burdett, James Young, Matt Rogerson, Amanda Wilhelm, Laura Bates.
Front row (left to right): Katie Carroll, Morgan Pel, Matt Hunt, Glenn Truelove, Sophie Jones, Matt Doughty, Anika Johnson, Ellen Stuart, Robbie McKenzie, Renée Malmo, Keshia Williams, (absent: Rebecca Courtney, Jonathon Coburn).

Front cover: Kimberly Brown (age 8)
Title page: Julian Hacquebard (age 7)
Back cover: Sophie Jones (age 7), Matt Hunt (age 7)
Introduction quote: Alex Fitzpatrick (age 7)

*Special thanks to Ann Stuart
for her kind assistance and interest in the book.*

Other books in the series:
A Child's Portrait of Shakespeare
Twelfth Night for Kids
A Midsummer Night's Dream for Kids
Romeo and Juliet for Kids
The Tempest for Kids
Hamlet for Kids
Much Ado About Nothing for Kids

Introduction

Rarely a day goes by when I am not amazed by what children can accomplish, given the challenge. As a Grade 2 teacher at Hamlet Public School in Stratford, Ontario, Canada, I have always been impressed by the openness and sincerity that seem to be a young child's natural attributes.

Over the past 20 years, I have introduced my classes to Shakespeare and his plays. For the children, Shakespeare has become a friend, not someone to be feared. His plays are looked upon as exciting stories, not drudgery. For me, Shakespeare is not an end in itself but a means to an end. His life and his plays have become a powerful medium for growth and development, especially in the area of language.

Each year, the class has worked together on one of Shakespeare's comedies. This year, we decided to study a tragedy—Macbeth. This book is the result of our journey. I chose to write the story in rhyme, as it is a medium children seem to particularly enjoy. The illustrations are by Grade 2 to Grade 6 students from Hamlet School. The stories are the imaginings of my Grade 2 class, pictured opposite. Their writing has been left in its unedited form and reveals the depth of the children's understanding of the characters and the inherent morality of the play itself. Who could capture the essence of Macbeth better than 7 year old Alex, below?

—Lois Burdett
Stratford, Ontario, Canada.

Macbeth is all about pride and blood and spears and swords but mostly it's about power. He started as a good and kind man who protekted his cuntry. He tried to become higher and mightyer but was never satisfied and became unsivillised.

Alex Gr. 2

THE CHARACTERS

The Royal Family

DUNCAN	King of Scotland
MALCOLM	Duncan's older son
DONALBAIN	Duncan's younger son

Lords and Ladies

MACBETH	Thane of Glamis
LADY MACBETH	Macbeth's wife
BANQUO	Macbeth's friend
FLEANCE	Banquo's son
MACDUFF	Thane of Fife
LADY MACDUFF	Macduff's wife
YOUNG MACDUFF	Macduff's son

ROSS	
LENNOX	Noblemen of Scotland
ANGUS	

OLD SIWARD	Earl of Northumberland
YOUNG SIWARD	Siward's son

Others

THREE WITCHES	
A SERGEANT	Duncan's attendant
A PORTER	Macbeth's servant
SEYTON	Macbeth's servant
MURDERERS	
A GENTLEWOMAN	Lady Macbeth's attendant
A DOCTOR	Macbeth's attendant
THREE APPARITION SPIRITS	
EIGHT APPARITION KINGS	

Elly
Vousden
(age 7)

I have a story from long ago,
A tale of misery, heartache and woe.
My play is glutted with hatred and greed,
And has a moral we all should heed.
So sit back my good friends, and I will unfold
A saga of passion that went uncontrolled.

I convey you to Scotland of yesteryear,
A place locked in combat, cruel and severe.
A country called Norway sent troops 'cross the sea.
The Scottish fought back to keep their land free.
Smoke and fire thickened the skies;
The air thundered with fierce battle cries.
The very ground shuddered with fright;
It really was a dreadful night.

Matt Charbonneau (age 9)

As the men battled with sword and shield,
Grey shadows appeared on the distant field.
"When shall we three meet again?
In thunder, lightning or in rain?"
"When the hurlyburly's done.
When the battle's lost and won."
"It is a matter of life and death,
And there we shall meet Macbeth."
"Fair is foul and foul is fair.
Hover through the fog and filthy air."
Then they raised their fists, their eyes ablaze,
And vanished into the gloomy haze.

Kate Vanstone (age 10)

Not far away, King Duncan did pace;
A worried look upon his face.
He cried out in anguish, "What is Scotland's fate?
Is there news of the battle that you can relate?"
Malcolm and Donalbain, the sons of the king,
Wondered too, how the action did swing.
They were with their father to lend their support
When a soldier staggered in with the latest report.
"What bloody man is this?" King Duncan cried.
"It's the sergeant who saved me!" Malcolm replied.

Kate Vanstone (age 10)

The soldier looked gaunt, with gashes to his head.
"Our victory was doubtful," he solemnly said.
"They outnumbered us and had fresh supplies.
The clammy air echoed with our dying cries.
Then in marched Macbeth, his sword held high.
He crossed the field, shouting curses to the sky.
For Scotland's honour he fought so well.
Before him many Norwegians fell,
And Sweno, their king, was forced to yield.
Then triumph was ours on that barren field.
But I am faint. My wounds cry to be seen."
"Quick," shouted the king, "let surgeons intervene."

Katie Carroll
(age 7)

Your majisty,
The start of the war was
not a sucess. Norway took
our best fighters. There
was deth as far as the eye
could see. But the battle
was not lost! Our tryumfint
hero Macbeth took Norway
by surprise! He brought fresh
men, for his fate was
Scotlands. Soon he reached
the dasterly King Sweno of
Norway and forced that nave
to surender. And peace was
Scotlands once more.

Glenn Truelove (age 8)

The Sergeant

9

As the soldier limped off, in came worthy Ross
With more news of the combat and a double-cross.
"King Duncan, I come from the battle at Fife
Where many a brave soldier lost his life.
The struggle seemed hopeless; their numbers were great,
And the Thane of Cawdor, we could not locate.
For he was a traitor and joined Norway's side.
Treachery and treason took away his pride.

Kate Vanstone (age 10)

Oh honerable king. I have some dredful news for you. Your Thane of Cawdor has turned from friend to foe. All his promises to you have been shatered. He has frowned on Scotland and joined the enemy's side. I know you believed in him but he is a big foney!

David Marklevitz (age 8)

King Duncan

10

But your thane of Glamis should be held in esteem.
In this terrible struggle, Macbeth was supreme.
He rallied his troops and he showed no fear,
Because of his bravery, our victory was clear."
King Duncan decreed, "Pronounce Cawdor's death!
With his former title, go greet Macbeth."
"Yes, my lord. I'll see it done.
"What Cawdor has lost, noble Macbeth has won."

Jonathon Baumunk
(age 8)

11

Back on the heath, the wind rose to a howl.
The air was heavy; the smell most foul.
Lightning shivered and thunder did sound.
The hags were hunched upon the cold ground.
"Where hast thou been?" the first witch cried.
"Killing swine," the second replied.
Then the third weird sister raised her head,
Her gnarled hands twisted and curled outspread.
"A drum," she croaked, "I hear a drum.
Listen, my sisters, Macbeth doth come."
"Thrice to thine and thrice to mine
And thrice again to make up nine.
Peace! The charm's wound up," they said,
Then peered into darkness straight ahead.

Shannon Campbell (age 9)

Macbeth appeared on the muddy path,
Wrapped in the storm's incredible wrath.
His good friend Banquo was by his side,
"How far to Forres?" Banquo cried.
Then he stopped short, "My eyes do betray."
The weird sisters barred their way.
Banquo wondered, "Am I beguiled?
What are these, so withered and so wild?"
Their icy stare gave Macbeth a chill.
"Speak!" he demanded. "It is my will!"

MACBETH

Just then something started to rise out of the marsh. One...two...then three wrincled hags apeared. They were awful ugly. Their hair Was tangled like a thorny bush. Dried blood covered their bony cheeks. Glowing red eyes snarled at Macbeth in an ungreeting Way. Macbeth backed away in horer. Finally he spoke, his lips showing fright. "Who are yee Women of life but yet look so ded?"

Story: Devon Searle (age 7)
Picture: Julian Hacquebard (age 7)

The silence was shattered as they rose one by one;
None of the sisters would be outdone,
"All hail, Thane of Glamis. Hail to thee!"
The first of the trio moaned with glee.
"Hail, Thane of Cawdor," the next squirmed to her feet.
Macbeth's heart faltered and missed a beat.
Then the third witch rose and quivered with laughter,
"All hail Macbeth, King of Scotland hereafter!"
These words thundered in Macbeth's brain,
What more in life was there to attain?

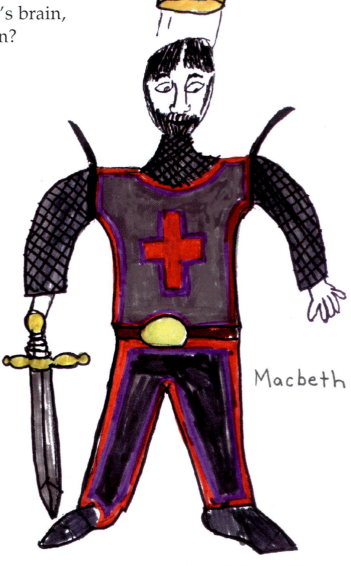

Me? The future King of Scotland?
It is more than I can
imagin. This has been a day
of victory! My spirits are lifted
and the suffering of war has
been pushed out of my brain
and is replaced by new hope.
My mind is at work, trying to
put together the puzzle.
                            Macbeth

Anika Johnson (age 7)

Macbeth

Stephen Marklevitz (age 11)

14

Macbeth seemed lost in a kind of trance.
Banquo gave his friend a worried glance,
"Why, my lord, do you fear words so sweet?
To be King of Scotland would be quite a treat!
I wonder what else these phantoms foresee!
What does the future hold for me?"
The sisters howled a bloodcurdling wail.
They circled Banquo and cried, "All hail!"
"Lesser than Macbeth, but greater," one muttered.
"Not so happy, yet happier," the next sputtered.
"You'll be father to kings," the last said with a frown,
"But Banquo, you'll never inherit the crown!"

Banquo

I am stunned by what I hear of Macbeth ...Glamis, Cawdor and yet to be king. The words of the three sisters ring in my mind. My sons and their sons will be rewarded with the crown. I have the promis of a row of kings. I am deeply trubled! I do not trust them at all!
                    Banquo

Morgan Pel (age 8)

Julian Hacquebard (age 7)

15

Macbeth bellowed in fury, "I charge you to stay!
From whence did you come? Tell us more, I say!
I am Thane of Glamis, by my father's death.
But Cawdor's thane lives! He still draws breath!
And to be crowned king is beyond belief.
We all know Duncan is Scotland's chief!
You imperfect speakers, a reply I demand!"
But like bubbles they melted into the land.
Macbeth gazed about, "Vanished into air?"
He pulled close his cloak. Had they really been there?

Caitlin More (age 11)

Just then, two messengers rode into view;
They greeted Macbeth, "Congratulations to you!"
"Glad tidings, brave general," Ross held out his hand.
"You're the greatest warrior in all our land.
And Thane of Cawdor! You've moved up the ranks!"
Angus agreed, "The King sends his thanks."
Macbeth was shocked. "What news they bring.
Two truths are told! Will I also be king?"
Already dark thoughts filled Macbeth's head;
His heart knocked his ribs and filled him with dread.
Then the spell he was under appeared to subside,
"I beg your forgiveness! I was preoccupied.
Dear friends, your goodwill is written on my heart,
And now, to His Majesty, we must depart.

Angus

Ross

Ashley Kropf (age 10)

17

Later, at Forres, there was quite a fanfare.
Duncan greeted his thanes in his chamber there.
"My brave Macbeth, I am in your debt.
Your gallant deeds, I will never forget."
Then he hugged Banquo in a hearty embrace.
Tears of joy flowed down Duncan's face.
He announced to his court, "And now for my heir!"
Macbeth's pulse quickened; he said a quick prayer.
But the king laid his hand on the head of his son,
"My eldest boy will be the one."
Macbeth felt faint; his heart turned to lead.
Duncan had picked Malcolm instead!
"The new Prince of Cumberland lies in my way;
I must act now! I cannot delay!
Stars, hide your fires!
Let not light see my black and deep desires!"

Evil thots fluster my brain. My conshense has no chanse against my will. I will be in charge of the whole land. And that means AllIllll of Scotland!

Macbeth

Story: Matt Hunt (age 7)
Picture: Rebecca Zehr (age 10)

Macbeth

Meanwhile, at home, his wife paced the room,
Shadowed by the castle's dreary gloom.
A letter arrived from her husband, Macbeth,
Containing a message of life and death.
Of strange events, Macbeth retold,
And glorious honours he did unfold.
She read the note, again and again,
Thrilling to its hidden refrain.
"Glamis thou art and Cawdor too,
Next, King of Scotland will be you!"
Ambition and power throbbed in her mind.
"And yet I fear my husband's too kind."
Then a servant arrived with more news to report,
"The king comes tonight with friends from his court."
"So soon," she gasped, "Oh harden my heart!
I'll force my husband to play his part."

Amber MaGill (age 9)

Dear beloved wife,

A very strange thing has happened to me. When I was marching proudly after the fight I came upon three hags. They looked like ghosts risen from the dead. They seemed so anchent and torn. After a few minutes of silence, they hailed me Thane of Glamis, Cawdor and King for evermore. I was stunned. My exsitement grows when I think on it. I am ankshus to meet the third proclamashon, and soon! There are many questions and many posabilitys. But dear wife leave the trubles behind. I will be home as soon as I can.

Macbeth

Anika Johnson (age 7)

19

Macbeth hurried home, as he had said.
Disturbing thoughts filled his head.
He burst through the door, breathless from his ride,
Then hastened to her room, to be by her side.
"Beloved wife, Duncan comes this eve."
Her eyes were like steel, "And when does he leave?
Your face is like a book, my lord;
You must hide your feelings," she implored.
"If, as you say, he comes tonight,
Duncan will not see the morning light!
I'll arrange it all, I guarantee.
Look after your guest; leave the rest to me!"

Lady
Macbeth

Dear Husband,
My ears have been on fire since I heard the news and my thots are icksploding in a swirling blaze. Just think if you are King I will be Queen. It will be the start of a great future.
Lady Macbeth

Story: Rebecca Courtney (age 7)
Picture: Megan Vandersleen (age 9)

20

By late afternoon, the king's party drew near.
King Duncan remarked, "Why it's beautiful here!"
Banquo agreed, "It's beyond compare!
Even the swallows love the sweet air."
The lady of the house greeted them with style,
"What's ours is yours!" she said with a smile.
As twilight fell, the castle was aglow;
Servants with torches rushed to and fro.
What a great celebration! What a jovial scene!
The court feasted 'til their platters were clean.

Kimberly Brown (age 9)

Macbeth couldn't stand it any more;
He rose from the table and rushed out the door.
"There is no reason to do this deed,
Just vaulting ambition, power and greed."
Macbeth was filled with shame and disgust,
"The king is here in double trust!
I'm his kinsman and subject, as well as his host;
I should protect him, to the utmost.
Yet to bear the knife is what I intend.
How could I do this to a friend?"

Oh the desishun, the desishun! I must take this one step at a time. My idea has gone too far. How can I kill for my sucess. The King is the brite summer days. He's the fresh kool rain. He is the world. And I am his loyal subjekt. There is no way I can do what I have planed. I can't bare the thot of it any longer. This is too much!
Macbeth

Ellen Stuart (age 8)

Julian Hacquebard (age 7)

Duncan knows nothing of my crushing thots. My mind is spining and I have a terable headake. I want to be king but Duncan has been so kind and gentle and treats me with respekt. There is so much love in the king's hart I cannot think of murdering him. I will go no further!
Macbeth

Rebecca Courtney (age 7)

22

Then Lady Macbeth appeared in the gloom,
"Why did you hurry from the room?"
"Duncan praises me highly," Macbeth said in despair.
"We'll proceed no further with this affair."
"Already," she mocked, "your resolve does fade?
You are a coward! You're just afraid!
My husband, you look so pitiful and pale."
Macbeth finally weakened, "But what if we fail?"
"I'll drug the guards! We will succeed!
Together, we will do the deed!
After his death, we'll display our grief,
Then my husband, you will be chief!"
"I will do as you ask and put on a show;
False face must hide what the false heart doth know."

Lady Macbeth

Why did you leave the
table? The King is
wundering where you
are. You should have
stayed put! This is not
like you! Be the same
Macbeth that saved
Scotland. Be brave and
do the deed. You my
lord will be the new
King!
              Lady Macbeth

Matt Hunt (age 7)

Ashley Kropf (age 10)

'Twas midnight when Duncan retired to his bed.
Morbid thoughts filled Macbeth's head.
He rushed outside to gather his wits,
His conscience screaming to call it quits.
Banquo and his son stood in the dim light,
Macbeth's arrival gave them a fright.
Banquo drew his sword and shouted, "Who's there?"
"A friend," said Macbeth, "Do not despair."
Banquo relaxed, "I've been with the king.
He sends to your wife this huge diamond ring."
Macbeth felt disgust at the thought of his crime,
"We could have done better if we had more time."
"I dreamt of the sisters," Banquo replied.
"I think not of them," Macbeth lied.
"We'll speak on this further, at a later date,
But let's get some rest. It's very late!"

Sophie Jones (age 7)

24

Macbeth stood alone and gazed into space;
A tormented look came over his face.
He saw a sight he couldn't believe,
And staggered back, "My eyes do deceive!"
A blood-stained dagger hung in midair,
Twisting, turning and taunting him there.
He lunged for it, yet his fingers passed through.
"Oh what in the world am I to do?
This false creation I cannot explain;
It holds such power over my brain.
But I waste my breath; the deed must be fulfilled.
With too many words, intentions are killed."

Ashley Kropf (age 10)

Ashley Kropf (age 10)

Is this a dagger I see before me? I grope for it but my hand goes throo. Yet still it floats. Now it is bludy not as before and sores like an eagle. Is this an illooshin of my mind? I cannot think strate. My ideas are driving me mad!

Macbeth

Laura Bates (age 7)

25

Just then, a bell tolled from the keep.
Macbeth shivered, "I hope Duncan is asleep!"
The summons filled his veins with fire,
And beckoned him to achieve his desire.
He crept like a shadow down the long, gloomy hall,
His mind no longer his at all.
His wife waited below, bold with greed.
"I've done my part. He's about the deed!"
The weapons were ready; everything was intact.
All that remained was the final act.

Matt Charbonneau (age 9)

Macbeth returned, a ghastly white,
"This is indeed a sorry sight!
These hands have taken the life of our king;
Nothing will heal their burning sting!
Through his chamber, I did creep,
A voice cried, 'Macbeth doth murder sleep!'
It was a sound I did abhor,
And still it cried, 'Sleep no more!'"
Lady Macbeth scoffed, "Just let it be!"
Her husband replied, "I will never be free!"
For in his efforts to reach his goal,
Macbeth had murdered his very soul.

My brain is no longer mine. I cannot cope with the mizery I have caused. I am filled with disgrace. If there is still life in the ashes of my crime I must go on but it seems imposible!

Macbeth

Morgan Pel (age 8)

Ashley Kropf (age 10)

His lady began to lose her cool.
"Why are carrying the daggers, you fool?
They're evidence," she continued to fume.
"You ought to have left them in the room!
Go smear the blood on each guard's face
They'll be suspected when the daggers are in place.
And wash that stain from off your hands.
If you're caught, it will ruin our plans.
Take them back now, I insist!
Hurry now or they'll be missed."

Macbeth what are you doing? You will be cot red handed! The dagers are evedence can't you see? Why do you stand as if chained to the ground? Your face is as white as snow. What is done is done and can't be undone. I demand you "TAKE THEM BACK AND NOW!"

Lady Macbeth

Matt Rogerson (age 8)

Megan Vandersleen (age 9)

28

Macbeth shook his head, "I'll go no more!
What I have done, I do deplore!"
"Then I'll do the job. I'm not fainthearted!"
She seized the daggers and quickly departed.
Macbeth heard knocking at the south gate,
It shattered the silence and did not abate.
He trembled with fear and paced to and fro,
"Why does each noise appal me so?"
Then his wife returned, her hands all red.
"They're of your colour," the Lady said.
We'll scrub and scour our hands all clean;
Duncan's blood will never be seen!"

Alison Dickens (age 9)

The deed is done. But oh, it leaves me in terror. I will never see the sweet face of King Duncan again. This is not what I bargined for. My mind will never rest. Darkness fills my head. It surrounds me with dred, and takes away my curage and freedom These thots will haunt me always and forever efect my brain. Duncan can never be awakined. He is in everlasting sleep. There is no way to free myself now. It is unchangeable!

                                        Macbeth

Anika Johnson (age 7)

The knocking continued at the castle gate.
The porter was in quite a state.
Finally, he staggered out of his chair,
"Who in the devil's name is there?
I'll open the door; I've had enough!"
There stood Lennox and the great Macduff.
"Good fellow," cried Macduff, "You're quite a sight."
"We were carousing, my lord, 'til late last night!"
"We're here," said Macduff, "to wake up the king."
In strode Macbeth; these words did sting.
"Welcome," he smiled. "I'll be your guide."
"We're grateful for that!" Macduff replied.

Ashley Kropf (age 10)

Macbeth led the way, his mind sunk in gloom.
He tried to sound cheerful, "Here is the room."
"Thanks again," said Macduff in a friendly tone.
"I'll take the liberty to go in alone."
Out in the hall, Lennox chatted away,
"Does His Majesty depart today?
And wasn't it a dreadful night?
The ground shook and trembled with fright.
Where we slept, our chimneys were blown down;
And mournful cries were heard all around!
The air was choked with sounds from the dead."
"'Twas a rough night," Macbeth quietly said.

Lennox

It has been a long and terable night. The world was turned upside down. The wind was howling owls were hooting and children wailed at the top of their lungs. Then "bam" in an instant everything was dethly silent. There must be a logical explanashon for this.

Lennox

Erin Bick (age 9)

Laura Bates (age 7)

A deafening scream pierced the air;
Macduff reeled from the chamber there.
"Oh horror! Horror! King Duncan is dead!
"Murder! Treason!" he cried in dread.
"Approach the King's room. Destroy your sight
With the cruelty of this plight."
Macbeth and Lennox hastened through the door.
Macduff continued to implore,
"Awake! Awake! Sound the alarm!
Who would do our king such harm?"
His voice thundered through the walls;
Nobles and servants rushed into the halls.

Macduff

Help awake! All is lost! When I went into the King's room I was bewildered with frite. I thot "the King sleeps too hevily?" I floo to him and did shake and shout. But try as I might he would not awake! It was a sorry site indeed.

Macduff

Story: Ellen Stuart (age 8)
Picture: Sophie Jones (age 7)

Bells rang out and torches flared.
Lady Macbeth dashed in, looking scared.
"Macduff," she screamed, "Tell me, I pray,
What is the cause of your dismay?"
"Oh gentle lady," was Duff's retort,
"'Tis not for you, this sad report."
Then, in a daze, he saw Banquo, his friend,
"His Majesty's life has come to an end.
King Duncan was murdered as he slept!"
"Oh villainous crime," Banquo wept.
Macbeth returned, "Life is worthless!" he cried,
Then in came the King's sons, side by side.

Erin Bick (age 9)

It was too awful to lay eyes on. Such a hidyus site. It was to blind myself when I went into Duncan's room. Evil hands have tuched our delikit king and he has disappeared into the darkness of another world. The thot of that is too much for me. This nightmare cannot be ekspresed in words. No one will be able to set him free now!

Macduff

Morgan Pel (age 8)

33

"What is amiss?" cried Donalbain.
Macduff replied, "Your father's been slain!"
Malcolm gasped, "Good Heavens! No!
Who would dare to strike the blow?"
"It appears his guards committed the deed!"
The noble Lennox did concede.
"Their weapons were bloody; their eyes were glazed,
They stared at us and were amazed."
"But I'm sorry," said Macbeth. "I went on a rampage,
I killed them both, in my terrible rage."

Julian Hacquebard (age 7)

Malcolm, Donalbain ... Your father the King is dead. All the good of the day is gone. No reashuring embrace will comfert you now. He has left this world forever. All eyes of Scotland will be clotted with tears of sadness and grey with mizery. I have seen many crimes but none as terible as this. Oh this night has held bitter deeds.

Macduff

Anika Johnson (age 7)

Macduff faced Macbeth, "Wherefore did you so?
You've destroyed the proof, don't you know?"
Macbeth's nerves were ready to break;
His lady knew that all was at stake.
She swayed in a faint. "Help me!" she cried.
"Look to the lady!" Macduff complied.
As the servants carried her away,
Banquo trembled in shock and dismay.
He held up his sword, "Hear me all!
I'll use my power. The guilty shall fall!"
Macduff continued, "We'll find who's to blame!"
Macbeth agreed, "I'll do the same!"

Macduff

Jennifer Stewart (age 7)

The sons of the king had no time to grieve
For they were getting ready to leave.
They whispered their plan in secret fear,
Worried that someone might overhear.
Malcolm shivered in the morning chill,
"Whose blood will be the next to spill?
Our father's murderer is not known,
And I am his heir, in line for the throne.
The lords all show grief, but is it real?
Or do they hide what they really feel?"

Dear Donalbain,
We are doomed if we stay in Scotland. I am afraid our own deth is near. There is no time to find the enemy. We must run! Run for our lives! I cannot think of what they may do.
                    Malcolm

Renée Malmo (age 7)

Malcolm

36

Nathan Rollerman (age 10)

"There's daggers in smiles!" Donalbain agreed.
Danger lurks here. We'd better take heed!
It would be no use," he told his brother,
"To kill one of us without the other.
We'll separate and say farewell,
To avoid our own death knell.
I will to Ireland quickly ride!"
"To England I'll journey," Malcolm complied.
The two embraced, broken-hearted,
And within the hour, they had departed.

Dear Malcolm,
Yes our lives are in danger.
There is no time to greave
for our father. We are not
safe in this land. I to
Ireland, you to England. If
we seperate it will be harder
to find us. We must leave
this place and now! Find your
horse and sadle it quickly.
Goodbye my brother. I will
miss you!
                    Donalbain

Donalbain

Keshia Williams (age 7)

And so the day passed, overwhelmed in gloom.
An old man and Ross spoke of great doom,
"In all my years, I must confess,
I have not seen such dire distress!"
"The time tells us," said Ross, "that day has begun,
Yet darkness remains and chokes out the sun."
Macduff appeared, "A rumour's been spread.
The sons are suspected for they have fled.
"Macbeth will be King!" the Thane of Fife sighed.
"The nobles have chosen. They'll not be denied.
Indeed, Macduff's words proved to be true.
At Scone, Macbeth made his royal debut!

Today was the crowning of our new King. The townspeople flooded the streets gathering food for the feast. Delicious smells filled the air and you could feel the exitement of the day. Sudenly a cheer went up and I saw Macbeth marching proudly through the castle gates. He was soon out of sight and I could only imagine what happened next.

Story: Anika Johnson (age 7)
Picture: Sophie Jones (age 7)

King
Macbeth

38

Banquo thought, "Now all is fulfilled,
Just as the fateful three had willed.
First Glamis, then Cawdor, and finally King,
My friend, Macbeth rules everything.
But I fear he played foully to take the crown,
And I could bring him crumbling down."
Macbeth arrived, looking regal indeed,
"A feast is planned, Banquo. Your presence we need."
Do you take your son Fleance riding today?"
"Yes, Your Majesty, and we mustn't delay,
But I'll return tonight, for your supper of state."
Macbeth thanked Banquo, "Please don't be late!"

Dear Diary
I cannot think of what my friend has done to inherit the highest throne of Scotland. One by one step by step he moves closer to my own deth. I do not like the look of this!
Banquo

David Marklevitz (age 8)

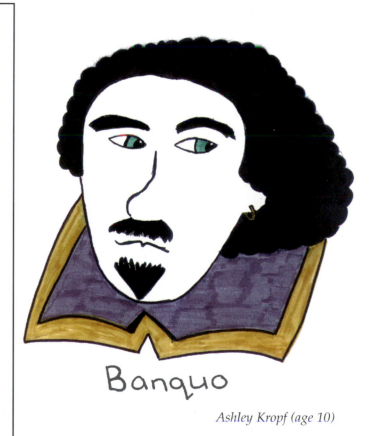

Dear Diary
All has been fufiled. We have been friends for a long time but I am becoming more suspishus each day. I do fear Macbeth has done the deed. He is no longer the same person I once knew. I hope I'm wrong. Could I be next?
Banquo

Matt Hunt (age 7)

Banquo

Ashley Kropf (age 10)

As Banquo departed, Macbeth paced the floor,
"There's not a man who I fear more!
His sons will rule. The witches have shown,
My life is empty, with no heir to the throne.
Have I lost my honour, so his sons will reign?
Have I stained my soul for Banquo's gain?
Never!" he cried. "I will challenge this fate!"
Then two ragged men arrived at his gate.
He told these murderers to ride very fast,
"You must not let Banquo or Fleance slip past!
If I'm to stay king, they both must die.":
"We'll do as you ask. Like the wind we'll fly!"

Kate Vanstone (age10)

For the royal couple, there was no peace of mind;
They now lived in terror and couldn't unwind.
The lady sighed, "We've achieved our desire.
Yet we now live in dread, of what might transpire.
Macbeth, why do you stay alone?
What's done is done! You have the throne!"
"Full of scorpions is my mind!
To treason and turmoil, I am resigned.
Banquo still lives, so I must proceed,
But, dearest wife, be innocent of the deed."
"Come, my good husband, be friendly and bright.
Enjoy your party and guests tonight!"
And at the feast, he was the perfect host.
Macbeth rose from his chair, "I propose a toast!"

Cassie Blackman (age 9)

All rise to the honer of the new KING MACBETH! Oh honerable friends let us drink to our happyness and peace forever. Let your trubles vanish and enjoy this merry feast. Let me hear the joyus clinking of goblets joining together to selabrate my new reign. Drink to your fill my cousins and let the warmth of the day soke into your mind Here, Here, let's eat!

Katie Carroll (age 7)

41

Out of the corner of Macbeth's eye,
He spied the murderers, cold and sly.
He left the table, then and there
To inquire about the grim affair.
"Is that blood upon on your face?"
"Yes, indeed. 'Tis Banquo's, Your Grace.
He died from the wounds to his head.
But, I'm sorry to say, young Fleance has fled."
Macbeth was distressed; that was plain,
Fear and resentment gripped his brain.

Megan Vandersleen (age 9)

Stephen Marklevitz (age 11)

42

My liege," said Ross, "if you are able,
Grant us your presence at the table."
"I'd love to," said Macbeth. "But where?
There seems to be no vacant chair."
Lennox replied, "Here is your spot.
Your Majesty, why do you look so distraught?"
Macbeth had turned a deathly white;
He shook and trembled at the sight:
Bloody Banquo was in his place,
A dreadful look upon his face.
The lords at the table saw nothing at all.
Macbeth shuddered and backed to the wall,
"I'm not to blame, can't you see!
Shake not thy gory locks at me!"

Ashley Kropf (age 10)

43

Ross leapt to his feet, "His Highness is ill!"
Lady Macbeth cried, "Gentlemen, be still!
He's had these attacks since he was a lad;
They make it appear he's going mad.
Sit, worthy friends! I pray you, remain.
As a new king, he's under great strain."
She took him aside, "You are a fool!
My husband, you look upon a stool!
For shame!" she hissed, "show you're a man!
Come back to the table. Stick to our plan."
The ghost dissolved into the air.
The lords were astonished, waiting there.

*Ashley Kropf
(age 10)*

Lady Macbeth

Macbeth what is the matter with you? It is your imaginashon! Do you want the banquet to be totally rooined? Relax! Behave yourself. You are embarasing me. You call yourself a man? More like a cowerdly snake! Now pull yourself together!
Lady Macbeth

Matt Hunt (age 7)

Macbeth strained hard to collect his wits,
"I'm sorry my friends; I'm prone to these fits.
Happiness and cheer, I do bestow!
He raised his glass, "To beloved Banquo!"
Then, he shrank back in dismay,
"Begone! Leave me alone I say.
Or approach like a tiger or bear in the night.
I'm not afraid if I can fight!"
Once again, the ghost's visit was brief.
"He's disappeared!" Macbeth sighed with relief.
Lady Macbeth announced, "The party is done!"
The guests left slowly, one by one.
Macbeth sat brooding, his thoughts far away.
"The Thane of Fife didn't come today.
I wonder if he's hatching some plot.
My spies will discover what I cannot.
Tomorrow, I'll meet the witches three,
And ask what they predict for me."

Banquo's ghost   Macbeth

Picture: Sophie Jones (age 8)
Story: Ellen Stuart (age 8)

I am teror stricken. All those blank eyes staring at my absense. It was there as plain as I have feet to stand on.... Banquo's ghost. He looked at me sternly strate in the eye and then he helped himself to my seat. I manijed to pull myself together. His angry smile glared at me and then he vanished into thin air. These aperishins of my mind threten me so.

Macbeth

The sisters were hidden in a cavern deep;
Around the cauldron, they did creep.
With their hands so crinkled with time,
They stirred a stinking, putrid slime.
"Double, double, toil and trouble,
Fire burn and cauldron bubble.
Fillet of a fenny snake,
In the cauldron boil and bake.
Adder's fork and blind worm's sting,
Lizard's leg and howlet's wing.
A horrid smell it does secrete,
Cool it now and the spell's complete.
By the pricking of my thumbs,
Something wicked this way comes."

Enchanted Broth

First collect from behind a snail
His slimy sticky disgusting trail

Then boil it quickly in a pot
Make sure the waters steaming hot.

Take the ring from the nose of a bull
Stir it only when the moon is full.

Add some venom and throw a fang in
Followed by a cobra's skin

When the concoction begins to froth
It will be enchanted broth.

Story: Patrick Henry (age 10)
Picture: Anika Johnson (age 7)

46

Macbeth strode in, "Answer my demand!
You secret hags. Where does my life stand?"
The witches shrieked, "Come, cauldron froth,
Shades of evil enchant this broth."
From the simmering pot rose an armoured head,
"Macbeth, beware Macduff!" it said.
The spirit dissolved into the steam.
A newborn child appeared like a dream,
"Be bloody, bold, fear not your death.
None of woman born shall harm Macbeth."
"Not of woman born? That's impossible you see.
Then the Thane of Fife has no power over me."

Julie Wilhelm (age 9)

The image faded and in its place,
There was another unusual face.
It was a child in a regal gown,
A branch in his hand and wearing a crown.
"Macbeth shall never vanquished be until
Great Birnam Wood meets Dunsinane Hill."
"I am invincible! All foes I'll confound.
We all know trees can't move around!
These powerful visions do assure
That, as King of Scotland, I am secure.
I'm deeply indebted and most impressed,
But I do have one final request.
Will Banquo's children rule after me?"
"Seek no more!" cried the witches three.

Rebecca Courtney (age 7)

Katie Carroll (age 7)

48

"Reveal it at once! I insist."
The hags conceded, and together hissed,
"Show his eyes and grieve his heart,
Come like shadows, so depart."
Majestic kings appeared in a row,
Carrying sceptres, their crowns aglow.
In single file, they marched past Macbeth.
His smile faded. He gasped for breath.
"They're all Banquo's. How can this be?
Four, five, six, that's seven I see.
Oh horrible sight! This I can't stand."
Then in came the eighth, a mirror in its hand.
Kings and more kings were reflected there.
"Does it ever end?" Macbeth cried in despair.
Banquo's ghost loomed at the end of the line.
He smiled as if saying, "These kings are all mine!"

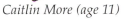

Caitlin More (age 11)

Ashley Kropf (age 10)

49

This was exactly what Macbeth had feared,
Then the witches and cauldron all disappeared.
Macbeth collapsed, then staggered to his feet
At the sound outside of a thundering beat.
He called for his man, who guarded the cave,
"Did you see the witches?" Macbeth sounded grave,
The guard answered, "Nothing, did I peruse,
Except men on horseback who brought you news.
Macduff is fled to England they say."
Macbeth was enraged, "No more delay!
Macduff has sealed his family's demise.
We'll take his castle by surprise
And order the death of his whole crew:
His wife, his babes, and his servants too."

Julian Hacquebard (age 7)

Macbeth's eyes groo bigger and bigger and his face turned a scarlit red His body started to shiver and shake. "Time has sliped thru my fingers. I will destroy Macduff, his family and anyone unlucky enuf to be at his castle. My chanse is now!!"

Katie Carroll (age 7)

50

Back at Fife, Lady Macduff was distraught,
"My husband's in England. He loves us not!
What had he done to make him fly the land?"
Ross consoled her, "Someone must take a stand!
Scotland is in a terrible way!
Under Macbeth, our freedoms decay.
Your husband does not deserve your blame.
But I take my leave. Words do inflame!"
The lady turned to her son, "Your father's a traitor."
"I don't believe you. He'll come back to us later."
Then a messenger arrived, "Danger is near!
I must leave now my lady. I can't be found here!"
But alas, the warning was delivered too late,
And all in the castle met a horrible fate.

Glenn Truelove (age 8)
Katie Carroll (age 7)
Ellen Stuart (age 8)
Anika Johnson (age 7)

THE FIFE DAILY

THANE'S FAMILY FOUND DEAD
Reporter: Glenn Truelove

The family of Macduff the Thane of Fife has been found dead in their home. They were descovered at 6:00 pm when a messenger arived at the casle. There was no sign of Macduff who was in England at the time. Vilegers are asked to take proper prokoshins until the murderers are found.

More on page 6

Photographer: Katie Carroll
Portrait of the Macduff family taken last year.

GARDEN PARTY CANSELLED
Reporter: Ellen Stuart

The garden party at the Macduff's casle has been canselled due to the resent tragidy. It was to be held April 23 in the Great Hall.

VEGETABLE STALL ROBBED
Reporter: Anika Johnson

April 22 a robbery was comitted in the market of Fife. A sack of potatoes, fifteen carrots and twenty pence were stolen. Anyone with informashin contact The Fife Daily

Vegitables

51

Meanwhile, Malcolm was in England's court.
Their king had offered his support.
Macduff arrived and urged Malcolm back,
Our poor country suffers. We must attack!"
Malcolm agreed, "We won't be delayed.
The brave, old Siward is mounting a brigade.
We'll march with him and ten thousand men,
And Scotland will be ours once again."
Just then, faithful Ross, rode in on his steed,
"I'm sorry to report another foul deed!"

Kate Vanstone (age 10)

"Despise not my tongue, for the news I bring,"
Ross added, "It's the work of the King!
Your castle was surprised," he solemnly said.
"Your family's been murdered! They are all dead!"
"My beloved wife? My little ones dear?"
And down his cheek there rolled a tear.
"Did you say all? My spirits droop.
All my pretty chickens, in one fell swoop?
That tyrant has a heart of stone!
Such sorrow I have never known."
Malcolm exclaimed, "Blunt not your heart,
Let grief change to anger and we will depart!"
Macduff rose in fury, "He'll die by my sword!
I'll get my revenge! To Scotland, my Lord!

Macduff

Ashley Kropf (age 10)

All of my little ones...killed
by the monstris Macbeth?
And my preshus wife too?
How can this be? It is
more than I can bare.
Why them? Whyn't I?
I am weak with sadness
heavy in misery. Nothing
can comfert me now!
              Macduff

David Marklevitz (age 8)

Meanwhile, Macbeth moved to Dunsinane Hill.
In the castle there, his wife was quite ill.
In the dead of night, through the halls, she'd creep;
Her eyes were open, yet she was asleep.
Her servant was horrified by this strange scene;
She called for the doctor to intervene,
"Here she comes, in her night attire;
She sees no one, but her brain is on fire!"
"We will note her mumblings," the doctor said.
But what they heard, filled them with dread.

Megan Vandersleen (age 9)

54

"Who knew he had so much blood," sighed the queen.
"Will these hands ne'er be clean?"
She rubbed them together in dismay,
"Yet here's a spot! Out I say!
All the perfumes will not sweeten this hand!"
The lady looked pale and could hardly stand.
"What's done cannot be undone!" she said.
Then she drifted off, "To bed! To bed!"
The doctor exclaimed, "I'm amazed by this sight.
I think, but I dare not speak tonight!"

Amber MaGill (age 9)

Rajdeep Nijjar (age 10)

Lady Macbeth

Oh these bitter hands. Will they ever be clean? I did not know that his blood would stain so. These hands hont me with the memery of the terible deed. All the lakes and rivers of the world cannot rid me of this blood. It is hopeless!
Lady Macbeth

Katie Carroll (age 7)

Now Scotland grew tired of Macbeth's cruel reign,
So the thanes all gathered, near Dunsinane.
They marched together toward Birnam Wood
And with the English army stood.
Malcolm greeted them with pleasure and pride,
"Thank you for fighting by my side.
Friends and kinsmen, the day is near
When our land will be safe and we'll live without fear.
Every soldier must cut a branch from the trees
And hide himself behind one of these.
We'll shadow our numbers as we move up the hill.
Macbeth won't guess our numbers still.
Together our armies will fight as one!
The battle for Scotland has just begun!"

Callyn Vandersleen (age 9)

Back in his castle at Dunsinane,
Macbeth prepared for war once again.
He was convinced he would never fall,
"Hang out our banners on the castle wall!
Let them desert me!" His rage was severe.
"Until Birnam Wood moves, I've nothing to fear!
Seyton, my armour, I demand!"
Then he called the doctor, who was close at hand.
"How is my wife feeling today?"
The doctor replied, "She's in a bad way!
She's not sick of body. It's all in her mind.
There is no cure that I can find!"

Sophie Jones (age 7)

Macbeth

I am afraid I cannot help the Queen. It is clear your wife is sufering from a strange madnes. You see Macbeth this dizeese is new to me and I cannot safely fix the problem. It is way beyond my powers.
Yours Sinsearly,
The Doctor

Matt Doughty (age 7)

My dear King
I don't know of this dizease. But I do know it is the vishon of the mind. I cannot cure her. This she will have to do herself. It is a distresing time.
The Doctor

David Marklevitz (age 8)

The screams of women filled the air,
But did not give the king a scare.
"Once I'd have cringed at such cries in my ear.
Now," he said, "there's nothing I fear."
Seyton announced, "The Queen is dead!"
"She should have died hereafter," Macbeth said.
"Life's a trivial tale, when all is done.
Each day rattles on, one by one.
Creeping closer and closer to dusty death."
Life had lost all meaning for Macbeth.

Macbeth

Death? What does it mean? Bits of love falling away till nothing is love any more. Death is distrukshen of the heart. Death is no friend of mine.
Macbeth

Ellen Stuart (age 8)

Ashley Kropf (age 10)

A terrified messenger burst through the door.
His face was pale as he crossed the floor,
"When I stood my guard upon the hill,
The trees of Birnam moved at will."
"Liar and slave! I'm not amused!
Trees don't walk. You must be confused!"
But the words of the spirits echoed in his brain,
"Fear not, 'til Birnam Wood meets Dunsinane."
Could it be true? Had he been misled?
"We'd better prepare!" was all that he said.
"Ring the alarm! We will attack!
At least we'll die with armour on our back!"

Anika Johnson (age 7)

Macbeth

*Jeremiah
Courtney
(age 9)*

Siward

Meanwhile, his enemies crept forward on cue,
Behind their branches, hidden from view.
"Throw down your screens," Malcolm cried.
"Soldiers, spread out far and wide.
Siward, advance your troops from the west.
Macduff and I will command the rest."
Siward's son found Macbeth first,
"Oh villainous tyrant! Your name I have cursed!"
"You can't harm me," Macbeth said with scorn.
"You, my friend, are of woman born!"
And though young Siward was brave and bold,
He was slain by Macbeth, as the vision foretold.

The soldiers closed in on Macbeth until he was surounded. Then out of the crowd of armer marched young Siward, looking strong and full of energy, with not one bit of fear in his body. They clashed together furiusly and the battle was on. Siward and Macbeth circled, lunged, ducked and brought their swords together, first slowly, then faster and faster until it all was a mass of metel. When the battle ended Siward lay dead at Macbeth's feet, a cruel smile on the tirant's face!

*Anika Johnson
(age 7)*

60

Then in came Macduff, across the field.
He spotted the king, "Turn, scoundrel! Yield!"
"Get thee back," Macbeth cried in disdain.
"Despair Macduff! Your fight is in vain.
You're of woman born. You'll never kill me.
I'm protected by a spell you see."
Macduff laughed in derision, "I'm not woman born.
From my mother's womb I was untimely torn."
The moment of truth had finally arrived,
In the duel that followed, only one survived.
Macbeth's body lay on the moor so bleak;
Too much glory he'd tried to seek.
He lost his castle, his army, his wife;
Ambition and greed cost him his life.

Matt Charbonneau (age 9)

So once more in Scotland, calm was restored;
Malcolm was crowned the country's new lord.
Duncan's son was a breath of fresh air;
He cared for his people and their welfare.
The crowds all cheered, "Hail to thee!"
From tyranny, they had been set free!
The fear and agony finally did cease,
And Scotland was once again at peace.

King
Malcolm

Sophie Jones (age 7)

62

What can we learn from this tale of strife,
As we make decisions in our life?
Don't lose your honour, as you reach for your dream,
Don't lose your virtue, your self-esteem.
Remember Macbeth; he wanted it all,
It brought a quick rise, but a swifter fall.
And worst of all, when he met his end,
Macbeth died without a single friend.

I know I'm not perfekt but it is better to be poor and troo than rich and false!
Ellen

Ellen Stuart (age 8)

You should always think before you leap and violence does not pay.
Glenn

Glenn Truelove (age 8)

Don't lisen to bad ecskuses. Trust your instinkts!
Rebecca

Rebecca Courtney (age 7)

There is more to this world then trying to get to the top. No one will weep at your grave.
Morgan

Morgan Pel (age 8)

Dulcie Vousden (age 7)

Lois's Grade 2 and 3 students prepare to perform Macbeth

Parents and Educators

This book can be used as a basis for a variety of activities either at home or in the classroom. Here are a few suggestions to use as a guideline.

- Play a version of the game "Grandmother's Trunk," creating a potion for the witches to throw in the cauldron. Children must remember the previous item and add one of their own.
- Assemble a glossary of words from the play such as apparition, cauldron, thane and so on.
- Post and discuss a Shakespearean Quote of the Day, such as "Fair is foul and foul is fair."
- Design a word search or crossword puzzle using the vocabulary and characters from the play.
- Write your own story about what happened after Shakespeare's play ended.
- Research the historical Macbeth and compare him with Shakespeare's character.
- Study a map of Scotland and draw places in the play such as Inverness, Forres and Scone.
- Act out the book as a reader's theatre with individuals taking on the various roles.
- Play a game of "Statues" with groups presenting a scene, such as the banquet.
- Design a coat of arms or banner for Duncan, Macbeth or Malcolm.
- Create your own spell to chant around the cauldron.
- Make a sound track, using voices, instruments, or recorded sound effects.
- Choreograph the entertainment at the coronation.

Educators who wish to arrange workshops or request permission to stage performances of *Macbeth for Kids* should contact the author: Fax: (519)273-0712 E-mail: lburdett@shakespearecanbefun.com